Grades 1–3

Open-ended Writing Activities for Young Children

WRITE a STORY

by Linda Beth Polon

Good Year Books

An Imprint of Addison-Wesley Educational Publishers, Inc.

Dedicated to

Shelia Solar, if it wasn't for her, I might not be writing

Philene and John Vaivods, the best of friends

Jill Conway, a magic wand waver

Laura Strom, my editor, who has been at the other end of the line when I needed advice

Letti and Jerry Sakai, two loving people

Truf, Phantom, Davey, Van Gogh, Motley, Mona Lisa, and Kai Kai, who have given their paws of approval on this book

Courtney McNeil, for her magic editing fingers on a computer

Good Year Books

are available for most basic curriculum subjects plus many enrichment areas. For more Good Year Books, contact your local bookseller or educational dealer. For a complete catalog with information about other Good Year Books, please write:

 Good Year Books
1900 East Lake Avenue
Glenview, IL 60025

Design: Street Level Studio
Illustrations: Street Level Studio
Text Copyright © 1998 Linda Beth Polon.
Illustrations Copyright © Addison-Wesley Educational Publishers, Inc.
All Rights Reserved.
Printed in the United States of America.

ISBN   0-673-36355-4

2 3 4 5 6 7 8 9 - PO - 04 03 02 01 00 99 98

Table of Contents

Write a Story 1-3, published by Good Year Books. Text Copyright © 1998 Linda Beth Polon.

Table of Contents *continued*

Write a Story 1-3, published by Good Year Books. Text Copyright © 1998 Linda Beth Polon.

How to Use This Book

Before starting this book, practice orally and in written form the alphabet with your children, as well as the writing and formation of some words.

It is a good idea to write a few whole-class or whole-group story dictations on a chalkboard so children can practice writing their letters, writing a sentence, and working on their spacing between words. For children who, in the beginning, are having trouble writing, have them dictate their stories to you. Write children's stories with a light marker so that they can trace over the words until they can work on their own.

Many of the stories include Word Banks. Children do not have to use all words in a Word Bank. They are provided to help spark ideas, not to limit content.

Many of the pages in this book contain a mini-lesson before the story starter. However, the last section contains story starters without mini-lessons. That section, as well as the last page with a list of additional story starters, offer the flexibility to reteach, reinforce, and strengthen skills your children should have already become familiar with. You can pre-assign a certain skill or skills for them to practice in their writing exercise.

An additional feature is the Writing Extensions, denoted by ▨. This is to be used at your discretion to further reinforce skills.

> Tip: Re-introduce the five senses to your children, explaining to them that describing the senses helps their stories come alive. Along with learning the importance of using adjectives, adverbs, and so on, learning the five senses and how they can be expressed are yet another tool for improving writing. This also might be the time to stress how important the opening sentence of a story should be. Let your children know that the more exciting and interesting the first sentence of a story is, the more a reader will want to read the rest of the story.

Name _____ **Date** _____

Look at the two pictures. Write, dictate, or copy a sentence about each picture. A sentence tells something. Remember that a sentence begins with a capital letter and ends with a period (.). A sentence must tell something, or it is not a sentence. Do not forget to color the pictures!

_____

_____

_____

_____

_____

_____

_____

Name _____ **Date** _____

Look at the two pictures. Write, dictate, or copy a sentence about each picture. Remember that a sentence begins with a capital letter and ends with a period (.). A sentence must tell something, or it is not a sentence. Do not forget to color the pictures.

_____

_____

_____

_____

_____

_____

_____

Name _____ **Date** _____

Look at the two pictures. Write, dictate, or copy a sentence about each picture. Remember that a sentence begins with a capital letter and ends with a period (.). A sentence must tell something, or it is not a sentence. Do not forget to color the pictures.

_____

_____

_____

_____

_____

_____

_____

Name _____ **Date** _____

Look at the two pictures. Write, dictate, or copy a sentence about each picture. Remember that a sentence begins with a capital letter and ends with a period (.). A sentence must tell something, or it is not a sentence. Do not forget to color the pictures.

_____

_____

_____

_____

_____

_____

_____

Name _____ **Date** _____

Look at the two pictures. Write, dictate, or copy a sentence about each picture. Remember that a sentence begins with a capital letter and ends with a period (.). A sentence must tell something, or it is not a sentence. Do not forget to color the pictures.

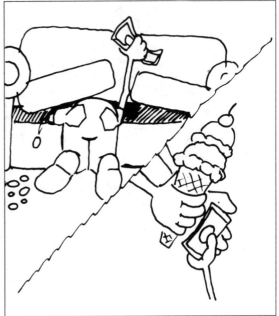

_____

_____

_____

_____

_____

_____

_____

Name _____ **Date** _____

Look at the two pictures. Write, dictate, or copy a sentence about each picture. Remember that a sentence begins with a capital letter and ends with a period (.). A sentence must tell something, or it is not a sentence. Do not forget to color the pictures.

_____

_____

_____

_____

_____

_____

_____

Name _____ **Date** _____

Look at the two pictures. Write, dictate, or copy a sentence about each picture. Remember that a sentence begins with a capital letter and ends with a period (.). A sentence must tell something, or it is not a sentence. Do not forget to color the pictures.

_____

_____

_____

_____

_____

_____

_____

Name _____ **Date** _____

Look at the two pictures. Write, dictate, or copy a sentence about each picture. Remember that a sentence begins with a capital letter and ends with a period (.). A sentence must tell something, or it is not a sentence. Do not forget to color the pictures.

_____

_____

_____

_____

_____

_____

_____

_____

Name _____ **Date** _____

Write a short story about the picture with three or more sentences that tell something. Remember each sentence begins with a capital letter and ends with a period (.). Write a title for your story. A title tells what your story is about. The first letter of each word in a title is capitalized, except little words, such as *a, the, an, and*. The first and last words in the title are always capitalized no matter how little they are.

The Birthday Surprise
The Day I Went to the Moon
I Had to Buy It

Also, the first word in your story should be indented. Use one finger space, and then begin your story. Remember not to write your words too close together. Do not forget to color the picture!

Title: _____

_____

_____

_____

_____

_____

 Writing Extension On another piece of paper, draw a picture and then write a story about it and title it using the rules above.

Write a Story 1-3, published by Good Year Books. Text Copyright © 1998 Linda Beth Polon.

Name _____ **Date** _____

Write a short story about the picture with three or more sentences that tell something. Remember each sentence begins with a capital letter and ends with a period (.). Write a title for your story. A title tells what your story is about. The first letter of each word in a title is capitalized, except little words, such as *a, the, an,* and. The first and last words in the title are always capitalized no matter how little they are.

Also, the first word in your story should be indented. Use one finger space and then begin your story. Remember not to write your words too close together. Do not forget to color the picture!

Title: _____

_____

_____

_____

_____

Writing Extension On another piece of paper, draw a picture and then write a story about it and title it using the rules above.

Name _____ **Date** _____

Write a short story about the picture with three or more sentences that tell something. Remember each sentence begins with a capital letter and ends with a period (.). Write a title for your story. A title tells what your story is about. The first letter of each word in a title is capitalized, except little words, such as *a, the, an, and*. The first and last words in the title are always capitalized no matter how little they are.

Also, the first word in your story should be indented. Use one finger space and then begin your story. Remember not to write your words too close together. Do not forget to color the picture!

Title: _____

_____

_____

_____

_____

 Writing Extension On another piece of paper, draw a picture and then write a story about it and title it using the rules above.

Name _____ **Date** _____

Write a short story about the picture with three or more sentences that tell something. Remember each sentence begins with a capital letter and ends with a period (.). Write a title for your story. A title tells what your story is about. The first letter of each word in a title is capitalized, except little words, such as *a, the, an, and*. The first and last words in the title are always capitalized no matter how little they are.

Also, the first word in your story should be indented. Use two finger spaces and then begin your story. Remember not to write your words too close together. Do not forget to color the picture!

Title: _____

_____

_____

_____

_____

Writing Extension On another piece of paper, draw a picture and then write a story about it and title it using the rules above.

Name _____ **Date** _____

Write a short story about the picture with three or more sentences that tell something. Remember each sentence begins with a capital letter and ends with a period (.). Write a title for your story. A title tells what your story is about. The first letter of each word in a title is capitalized, except little words such as *a, the, an, and*. The first and last words in the title are always capitalized, no matter how little they are.

Also, the first word in your story should be indented. Use one finger space and then begin your story. Remember not to write your words too close together. Do not forget to color the picture!

Title: _____

_____

_____

_____

_____

 Writing Extension On another piece of paper, draw a picture and then write a story about it and title it using the guidelines above.

Warm-up Write-a-Story Activities

Name _____ **Date** _____

Write a short story about the picture with three or more sentences that tell something. Remember each sentence begins with a capital letter and ends with a period (.). Write a title for your story. A title tells what your story is about. The first letter of each word in a title is capitalized, except little words, such as *a, the, an, and*. The first and last words in the title are always capitalized no matter how little they are.

Also, the first word in your story should be indented. Use one finger space and then begin your story. Remember not to write your words too close together. Do not forget to color the picture!

Title: _____

_____

_____

_____

_____

Writing Extension On another piece of paper, draw a picture and then write a story about it and title it using the guidelines above.

Name _____ **Date** _____

Write a short story about the picture with three or more sentences that tell something. Remember each sentence begins with a capital letter and ends with a period (.). Write a title for your story. A title tells what your story is about. The first letter of each word in a title is capitalized, except little words, such as *a, the, an, and*. The first and last words in the title are always capitalized no matter how little they are.

Also, the first word in your story should be indented. Use one finger space and then begin your story. Remember not to write your words too close together. Do not forget to color the picture!

Title: _____

_____

_____

_____

_____

 Writing Extension On another piece of paper, draw a picture and then write a story about it and title it using the guidelines above.

Write a Story 1-3, published by Good Year Books. Text Copyright © 1998 Linda Beth Polon.

Warm-up Write-a-Story Activities

Name _____ **Date** _____

Write a short story about the picture with three or more sentences that tell something. Remember each sentence begins with a capital letter and ends with a period (.). Write a title for your story. A title tells what your story is about. The first letter of each word in a title is capitalized, except little words, such as *a, the, an, and*. The first and last words in the title are always capitalized no matter how little they are.

Also, the first word in your story should be indented. Use one finger space, and then begin your story. Remember not to write your words too close together. Do not forget to color the picture!

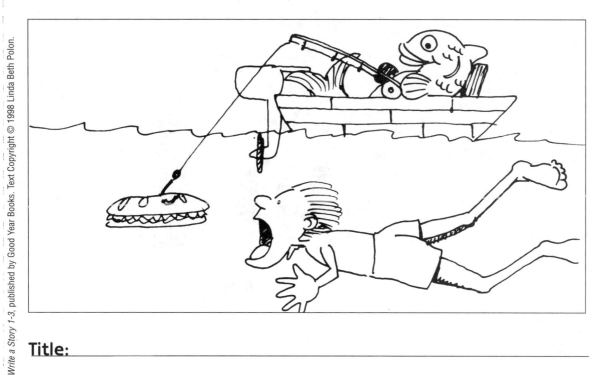

Write a Story 1-3, published by Good Year Books. Text Copyright © 1998 Linda Beth Polon.

Title: _____

_____

_____

_____

_____

 Writing Extension On another piece of paper, draw a picture and then write a story about it and title it using the guidelines above.

Name _____ **Date** _____

Write a short story about the picture with three or more sentences that tell something. Remember each sentence begins with a capital letter and ends with a period (.). Write a title for your story. A title tells what your story is about. The first letter of each word in a title is capitalized, except little words, such as *a, the, an, and.* The first and last words in the title are always capitalized no matter how little they are.

Also, the first word in your story should be indented. Use one finger space and then begin your story. Remember not to write your words too close together. Do not forget to color the picture!

Title: _____

_____

_____

_____

_____

 Writing Extension On another piece of paper, draw a picture and then write a story about it and title it using the guidelines above.

Write a Story 1–3, published by Good Year Books. Text Copyright © 1998 Linda Beth Polon.

Name _____ **Date** _____

Write a short story about the picture with three or more sentences that tell something. Remember each sentence begins with a capital letter and ends with a period (.). Write a title for your story. A title tells what your story is about. The first letter of each word in a title is capitalized, except little words, such as *a, the, an, and.* The first and last words in the title are always capitalized no matter how little they are.

Also, the first word in your story should be indented. Use one finger space and then begin your story. Remember not to write your words too close together. Do not forget to color the picture!

Title: _____

_____

_____

_____

_____

_____

Writing Extension On another piece of paper, draw a picture and then write a story about it and title it using the guidelines above.

Name _____ **Date** _____

Write a short story about the picture with three or more sentences that tell something. Remember each sentence begins with a capital letter and ends with a period (.). Write a title for your story. A title tells what your story is about. The first letter of each word in a title is capitalized, except little words, such as *a, the, an,* and. The first and last words in the title are always capitalized no matter how little they are.

Also, the first word in your story should be indented. Use one finger space and then begin your story. Remember not to write your words too close together. Do not forget to color the picture!

Title: _____

_____

_____

_____

_____

_____

Writing Extension On another piece of paper, draw a picture and then write a story about it and title it using the guidelines above.

Name _____ **Date** _____

Write a short story about the picture with three or more sentences that tell something. Remember each sentence begins with a capital letter and ends with a period (.). Write a title for your story. A title tells what your story is about. The first letter of each word in a title is capitalized, except little words, such as *a, the, an, and*. The first and last words in the title are always capitalized no matter how little they are.

Also, the first word in your story should be indented. Use one finger space and then begin your story. Remember not to write your words too close together. Do not forget to color the picture!

Title: _____

_____

_____

_____

_____

_____

 Writing Extension On another piece of paper, draw a picture and then write a story about it and title it using the guidelines above.

Name _____ **Date** _____

Write a short story about the picture with three or more sentences that tell something. Remember each sentence begins with a capital letter and ends with a period (.). Write a title for your story. A title tells what your story is about. The first letter of each word in a title is capitalized, except little words, such as *a, the, an,* and. The first and last words in the title are always capitalized no matter how little they are.

Also, the first word in your story should be indented. Use one finger space and then begin your story. Remember not to write your words too close together. Do not forget to color the picture!

<u>Title:</u> _____

_____

_____

_____

_____

_____

 Writing Extension On another piece of paper, draw a picture and then write a story about it and title it using the guidelines above.

Name _____ **Date** _____

Write a short story about the picture with three or more sentences that tell something. Remember each sentence begins with a capital letter and ends with a period (.). Write a title for your story. A title tells what your story is about. The first letter of each word in a title is capitalized, except little words, such as *a, the, an, and*. The first and last words in the title are always capitalized no matter how little they are.

Also, the first word in your story should be indented. Use two finger spaces and then begin your story. Remember not to write your words too close together. Do not forget to color the picture!

Title: _____

_____

_____

_____

_____

_____

 Writing Extension On another piece of paper, draw a picture and then write a story about it and title it using the guidelines above.

Name _____ **Date** _____

Write a short story about the picture with three or more sentences that tell something. Remember each sentence begins with a capital letter and ends with a period (.). Write a title for your story. A title tells what your story is about. The first letter of each word in a title is capitalized, except little words, such as *a, the, an,* and. The first and last words in the title are always capitalized no matter how little they are.

Also, the first word in your story should be indented. Use one finger space and then begin your story. Remember not to write your words too close together. Do not forget to color the picture!

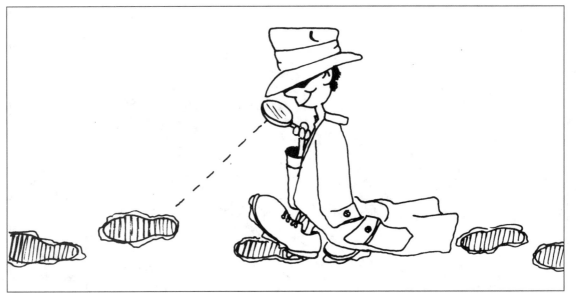

Title: _____

_____

_____

_____

_____

_____

 Writing Extension On another piece of paper, draw a picture and then write a story about it and title it using the guidelines above.

Write a Story 1–3, published by Good Year Books. Text Copyright © 1998 Linda Beth Polon.

Name _____ **Date** _____

Write a short story about the picture with three or more sentences that tell something. Remember each sentence begins with a capital letter and ends with a period (.). Write a title for your story. A title tells what your story is about. The first letter of each word in a title is capitalized, except little words, such as *a, the, an, and.* The first and last words in the title are always capitalized no matter how little they are.

Also, the first word in your story should be indented. Use one finger space and then begin your story. Remember not to write your words too close together. Do not forget to color the picture!

Title: _____

_____

_____

_____

_____

_____

_____

Writing Extension On another piece of paper, draw a picture and then write a story about it and title it using the guidelines above.

Name _____ **Date** _____

Write a short story about the picture with three or more sentences that tell something. Remember each sentence begins with a capital letter and ends with a period (.). Write a title for your story. A title tells what your story is about. The first letter of each word in a title is capitalized, except little words, such as *a, the, an,* and. The first and last words in the title are always capitalized no matter how little they are.

Also, the first word in your story should be indented. Use one finger space and then begin your story. Remember not to write your words too close together. Do not forget to color the picture!

Title: _____

_____

_____

_____

_____

_____

 Writing Extension On another piece of paper, draw a picture and then write a story about it and title it using the guidelines above.

Write a Story 1–3, published by Good Year Books. Text Copyright © 1998 Linda Beth Polon.

Name _____ Date _____

Look at the picture. Write or dictate a short story about it. Use some words from the word bank as well as words of your own. Make sure you have capitalized all words that need to be capitalized. Other than the first word in a sentence, remember to capitalize proper names. Proper names name things, such as the names of people and pets, companies and buildings, books and movies, cities, states, countries, planets, products, days of the week, months, holidays, and street names. Initials should also be capitalized.

Word Bank

gail • games galore store • sunday • mr. mcNeil • sunset street • october • halloween • museum of science and industry • gorham apts. • choco chocolate candy

Title: _____

_____

_____

_____

_____

_____

_____

_____

_____

_____

Writing Extension On another piece of paper, draw and color a picture and then write about it. This time you will not be given a word bank, so include as many words as you can that must be capitalized.

Name _____ Date _____

Look at the picture. Write or dictate a short story about it. Use some words from the word bank as well as words of your own. Make sure you have capitalized all words that need to be capitalized. Other than the first word in a sentence, remember to capitalize proper names. Proper names name things, such as the names of people and pets, companies and buildings, books and movies, cities, states, countries, planets, products, days of the week, months, holidays, and street names. Initials should also be capitalized.

Word Bank

laurie • motley (pet) • wednesday • edie • phil's TV mart • seattle • smith's computer school • july • washington • mrs. wolff • be kind pet store

Title:_____

_____

_____

_____

_____

_____

_____

_____

_____

Writing Extension On another piece of paper, draw and color a picture and then write about it. This time you will not be given a word bank, so include as many words as you can that must be capitalized.

Write a Story 1–3, published by Good Year Books. Text Copyright © 1998 Linda Beth Polon.

Name _____ **Date** _____

Look at the picture. Write or dictate a short story about it. Use some words from the word bank as well as words of your own. Make sure you have capitalized all words that need to be capitalized. Other than the first word in a sentence, remember to capitalize proper names. Proper names name things, such as the names of people and pets, companies and buildings, books and movies, cities, states, countries, planets, products, days of the week, months, holidays, and street names. Initials should also be capitalized.

Word Bank

los angeles • february • save away market • england • tim • hannah • tuesday • the lion king • california • miss peters • canada • valentine's day

Title: _____

_____

_____

_____

_____

_____

_____

_____

_____

 **Writing Extension** On another piece of paper, draw and color a picture and then write about it. This time you will not be given a word bank, so include as many words as you can that must be capitalized.

Write a Story 1–3, published by Good Year Books. Text Copyright © 1998 Linda Beth Polon.

Name _____ **Date** _____

Look at the picture. Write or dictate a short story about it. Use some words from the word bank as well as words of your own. Make sure you have capitalized all words that need to be capitalized. Other than the first word in a sentence, remember to capitalize proper names. Proper names name things, such as the names of people and pets, companies and buildings, books and movies, cities, states, countries, planets, products, days of the week, months, holidays, and street names. Initials should also be capitalized.

Word Bank

christmas • disneyland • ramon • december • sunday • vilma • bob • united states • u.s.a.

Title: _____

_____

_____

_____

_____

_____

_____

_____

_____

_____

 Writing Extension On another piece of paper, draw and color a picture and then write about it. This time you will not be given a word bank, so include as many words as you can that must be capitalized.

Write a Story 1-3, published by Good Year Books. Text Copyright © 1998 Linda Beth Polon.

Warm-up Write-a-Story Activities

Name _____ **Date** _____

Look at the picture. Write or dictate a short story about it. Use some words from the word bank as well as words of your own. Make sure you have capitalized all words that need to be capitalized. Other than the first word in a sentence, remember to capitalize proper names. Proper names name things, such as the names of people and pets, companies and buildings, books and movies, cities, states, countries, planets, products, days of the week, months, holidays, and street names. Initials should also be capitalized.

Word Bank

brentwood school • san vicente blvd. • fourth of july • august • greato movie theater • peanuts (book) • saturday • hal • eddie • diet zippo soda

Title: _____

_____

_____

_____

_____

_____

_____

_____

_____

Writing Extension On another piece of paper, draw and color a picture and then write about it. This time you will not be given a word bank, so include as many words as you can that must be capitalized.

Name _____ **Date** _____

Look at the picture. Write or dictate a short story about it. Use some words from the word bank as well as words of your own. Make sure you have capitalized all words that need to be capitalized. Other than the first word in a sentence, remember to capitalize proper names. Proper names name things, such as the names of people and pets, companies and buildings, books and movies, cities, states, countries, planets, products, days of the week, months, holidays, and street names. Initials should also be capitalized.

Word Bank

father's day • mother's day • march • new york • statue of liberty • friday • easter • passover • besta's pizzeria restaurant • mexico

Title: _____

_____

_____

_____

_____

_____

_____

_____

_____

_____

Write a Story 1–3, published by Good Year Books. Text Copyright © 1998 Linda Beth Polon.

 Writing Extension On another piece of paper, draw and color a picture and then write about it. This time you will not be given a word bank, so include as many words as you can that must be capitalized.

Name _____ **Date** _____

One sentence you know how to write is a telling sentence—one that tells something and begins with a capital letter and ends with a period (.). Another kind of sentence is an asking sentence or a question, which begins with a capital letter and ends with a question mark (?). An example of a question is "How do you feel?"

Look at the four pictures and write four questions for each one. (Two questions are done for you under the first picture.)

1. Why is the girl smiling?

2. Is the girl going to a party today?

3.

4.

1.

2.

3.

4.

1.

2.

3.

4.

1.

2.

3.

4.

Punctuation

Name _____ **Date** _____

An exclamation is another kind of sentence you can use in your stories. This kind of sentence shows strong, emotional feelings such as happiness, excitement, or anger. An exclamation ends with an exclamation point (!). An example of an exclamation is "I got a baby kitten!" Look at the four pictures and write four exclamation sentences for each one. (Two exclamation sentences are done for you under the first picture.)

1. My mom is going to have a baby!   1.

2. I lost my homework!   2.

3.   3.

4.   4.

1.   1.

2.   2.

3.   3.

4.   4.

Punctuation

Name _____ Date _____

Another kind of sentence to be used in your stories is a command, and it ends with a period (.). A command sentence gives an order. It tells someone to do something. An example of a command is "Hang up your clothes before going out to play." Look at the four pictures and write four command sentences for each one. (Two command sentences are done for you under the first picture.)

1. Clean out your desk.

2. Stop talking.

3.

4.

1.

2.

3.

4.

1.

2.

3.

4.

1.

2.

3.

4.

Write a Story 1–3, published by Good Year Books. Text Copyright © 1998 Linda Beth Polon.

Punctuation

Name _____ **Date** _____

Look at the pictures and write a short story about each one with a title. Use the first word bank to help you write about the first picture. When you are done writing your story, reread it and see if you can find telling sentences, asking sentences, exclamation sentences, and command sentences. If so, underline them. If not, try rewriting to add some. Continue on a separate piece of paper, if necessary.

First Word Bank

home • backyard • room • food • happy • sad • dinner • TV • talk • brother • sister • share • toys • games • playing

Title: _____

_____

_____

_____

_____

_____

Writing Extension: On a separate piece of paper, write a story about the second picture, using the second word bank and the guidelines above.

Second Word Bank

pretend • movie star • TV star • teacher • artist • writer • doctor • computer expert • airplane pilot • grown-up • why • because

Name _____ **Date** _____

Use the words in the word bank to help you write a story about the picture. Try to include some telling sentences, asking sentences, exclamation sentences, and command sentences.

Word Bank

outer space • aliens • planets • astronaut • blast-off • scary • blackness • world • Venus • Mars • Jupiter • Earth • Uranus • Saturn • Pluto • spaceship • satellite • camera • view • feelings • outfit • heavy • food • lightness

Title: _____

_____

_____

_____

_____

_____

_____

_____

_____

_____

_____

_____

_____

_____

_____

Write a Story 1-3, published by Good Year Books. Text Copyright © 1998 Linda Beth Polon.

Name _____ **Date** _____

Review the comma rules below then look at the picture and write a story. Include some commas (,) in your story. A comma is needed because sometimes when you write, you need to take a little rest, or pause, between words to make your sentences clearer and sound better.

When should you use a comma?

1. Use a comma when you begin a sentence with the word yes, no, OK, or well. (Yes, I'll come to your house.)

2. Use a comma when you begin or end a sentence with someone's name. (Laurie, where is my toy? I'll be at the market, Juan.)

3. Use a comma when you write three or more nouns or proper nouns in a row. (I have a kitten, a puppy, a parakeet, and a dog. My best friends are Edie, Annette, Don, and Janet.)

4. Use a comma when you write two complete sentences with the word and in the middle. (Lisette went to the pet store, and Maria went to school.)

_____

_____

_____

_____

_____

_____

Punctuation

Name _____ **Date** _____

Look at the two sets of stories. Each one has three pictures, but they are out of story order (sequence) in telling what happened first, second, and last in the stories. A story must have a beginning, middle, and ending. Place the two sets of pictures in story order by writing 1, 2, or 3 in the small box in the pictures. Then write the sentences in correct story order.

The dog came back with the ball.   The girl threw the ball.   The dog ran after it.

1. _____

2. _____

3. _____

She felt full and happy.   She ate the hamburger.   The girl was hungry.

1. _____

2. _____

3. _____

Sequence

Name _____ **Date** _____

Look at the two sets of stories. Each one has three pictures, but they are out of story order (sequence) in telling what happened first, second, and last in the stories. A story must have a beginning, middle, and ending. Place the two sets of pictures in story order by writing 1, 2, or 3 in the small box in the pictures. Then write the sentences in correct story order.

The bee found her home. A sad bee looked for her home. The bee was happy.

1. _____

2. _____

3. _____

 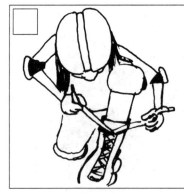 

The girl raced down the street. The girl put on her skates. The girl's skates were under the bed.

1. _____

2. _____

3. _____

Write a Story 1-3, published by Good Year Books. Text Copyright © 1998 Linda Beth Polon.

Sequence

Name _____ **Date** _____

Below are two sets of three boxes with pictures in correct story order. Write a sentence or two to begin your story under Box 1. Under Box 2, write the middle part of your story. Under Box 3, write your ending.

_____   _____   _____

_____   _____   _____

_____   _____   _____

_____   _____   _____

_____   _____   _____

_____   _____   _____

_____   _____   _____

_____   _____   _____

 Writing Extension On a separate piece of paper, draw three boxes and write and illustrate your own story using the directions above.

Sequence

Name _____ **Date** _____

Match the first part of the sentences on the left (the subjects) with the rest of the sentences on the right (their predicates) to make a telling sentence. (Remember if a sentence does not tell anything, it is not a sentence.) The subject tells who or what the sentence is talking about. The predicate tells what the subject is doing.

After matching the subjects with their predicates below, write a story using some of these sentences. Then underline the subject or subjects in each of your sentences. Illustrate your story on a separate piece of paper.

1) The girl   screamed.

2) The baby   drove fast and could not stop.

3) The red car   raced on her skateboard.

4) Many rocks   was on the sidewalk.

5) My mother   were in front.

Title: _____

_____

_____

_____

_____

_____

_____

_____

Parts of Speech

Name _____ **Date** _____

Match the first part of the sentences on the left (the subjects) with the rest of the sentences on the right (their predicates) to make a telling sentence. (Remember if a sentence does not tell anything, it is not a sentence.) The subject tells who or what the sentence is talking about. The predicate tells what the subject is doing.

After matching the subjects with their predicates below, write a story using some of these sentences. Then underline the subject or subjects in each of your sentences. Illustrate your story on a separate piece of paper.

1) The children and their friends   laid on their eggs.

2) The cow   had a big farm.

3) The horse   mooed loudly.

4) The pigs   played with the animals.

5) The farmer and his wife   ate hay.

6) The chicken and the duck   rolled in the mud.

Title: _____

_____

_____

_____

_____

_____

_____

_____

Name _____ **Date** _____

Color the picture, write a story about it, and add a title. Many times a sentence has one subject and a predicate, for example, "The zebra was lost." Sometimes there are two sentences joined together with a comma and the word *and*. Each of these two sentences has its own subject and predicate. This is called a compound sentence. For example, "The rabbit hopped, and the frog jumped on the rock."

When you are finished with your story, see if you wrote any compound sentences. If you did, underline them. If you didn't, revise your story so that you have at least one compound sentence.

Title: _____

_____

_____

_____

_____

_____

 Writing Extension On another piece of paper, write a story with at least three compound sentences and illustrate it, following the guidelines above.

Parts of Speech

Name _____ **Date** _____

Now it is time to write your stories adding describing words called **adjectives**. Adjectives are words that tell more about other nouns. Adjectives make your stories more real and exciting. Some examples are *large* ball, *fluffy* cat, *curly* hair, *kind* Ms. Wondra, *half* moon, *yellow* house, and *smooth* table.

Look at the picture. Use some of the adjectives in the first word bank plus your own adjectives to write a story with a title.

First Word Bank

long • old • brown • smiling • friendly • short • hot • crying • simple • young • funny

Title: _____

_____

_____

_____

_____

_____

 Writing Extension   On another piece of paper, draw a picture, color it, and then write a story using the adjectives in the second word bank plus your own.

Second Word Bank

wet • soft • hard • cold • drippy • new • good • beautiful • sweet • mushy • difficult

Name _____ **Date** _____

Look at the picture. Write a story with a title using as many of the adjectives in the first word bank as you would like plus your own adjectives.

First Word Bank

twisted • slow • straight • wrinkled • smelly • tight • kind • tall • thin • fuzzy • cute

Title: _____

_____

_____

_____

_____

_____

_____

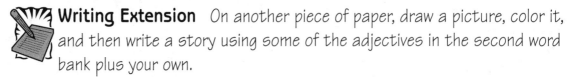 **Writing Extension** On another piece of paper, draw a picture, color it, and then write a story using some of the adjectives in the second word bank plus your own.

Second Word Bank

juicy • thick • round • square • wide • great • sticky • tasty • shiny • wonderful • super • skinny • tiny

Write a Story 1-3, published by Good Year Books. Text Copyright © 1998 Linda Beth Polon.

Name _____ **Date** _____

Write a story from the story idea list below. Add a title and then illustrate your story on a separate sheet of paper. To make your story more interesting, you should use many adjectives. After writing your story, count how many adjectives you used and write that number at the end of your story.

Story ideas: school • home • friends • a free shopping spree in a toy store • an airplane trip to anywhere • good things you do for people you know • if I became invisible

Title: _____

_____

_____

_____

_____

_____

_____

_____

_____

_____

_____

_____

_____

Name _____ **Date** _____

Sometimes two or more adjectives (describing words) can mean the same thing. These adjectives are called synonyms. A synonym is a word that means the same as another word in that language. (For example, <u>small</u>/<u>little</u> kitten, <u>easy</u>/ <u>simple</u> homework, <u>difficult</u>/ <u>hard</u> cleaning, and <u>large</u>/ <u>big</u> present)

Look at the picture and write a story with a title. Afterward, write a synonym for each adjective you use. Write the adjectives and their synonyms at the bottom of your page. For example, for the sentence "I saw the skinny man," you would write "skinny/thin" at the bottom of the page.

Title: _____

_____

_____

_____

_____

_____

_____

_____

Write a Story 1-3, published by Good Year Books. Text Copyright © 1998 Linda Beth Polon.

Parts of Speech

Name _____ **Date** _____

A verb is an action word found in the predicate part of a sentence. The verb tells what the subject is doing. (For example, "The cat <u>jumps</u> over the dog.") Some verbs are more exciting than others. (For example, laugh/<u>giggle</u>, run/<u>race</u>, stayed/<u>froze</u>, drove/<u>sped</u>) Look at the picture and write a story with a title. Use as many exciting verbs as you can.

Title: _____

_____

_____

_____

_____

_____

_____

 Writing Extension On another piece of paper, write a story with a title using exciting verbs in most of your sentences. Do not forget to draw and color a picture.

Write a Story 1–3, published by Good Year Books. Text Copyright © 1998 Linda Beth Polon.

Parts of Speech

Name _____ **Date** _____

An adverb is a word that describes a verb, an adjective, or another adverb. Adverbs tell more about the word they are describing. For example, "Mom smiled beautifully" tells how Mom smiled. Adverbs are not required in every sentence, but they do add more detail to your story.

Look at the picture. Write a story about it and add a title. Check each verb you used to see if it has an adverb near it. For this exercise, add an adverb for each verb in your story.

Title: _____

_____

_____

_____

_____

_____

Writing Extension On a second piece of paper, write another story using verbs and adverbs. Make sure you have used adverbs. If not, revise your story by adding adverbs wherever appropriate. Do not forget to draw and color a picture and add a title.

Write a Story 1-3, published by Good Year Books. Text Copyright © 1998 Linda Beth Polon.

Parts of Speech

Name _____ **Date** _____

Look at the picture and write a story with a title. In your story make as many of your nouns (persons, places, or things) plural as possible. (*Plural* means "more than one.") The words in the first word bank become plural by adding the letter s at the end of the word (for example: teacher<u>s</u>, day<u>s</u>). You may use the words in the first word bank in your story. Do not forget to add a title and to draw and color a picture.

First Word Bank

friend • school • day • balloon • team • teacher • visitor • yard • classmate • room • chair

Title: _____

_____

_____

_____

_____

_____

_____

_____

_____

_____

 Writing Extension On a separate sheet of paper, write a story using the second word bank. Make as many of your nouns plural as possible. Do not forget to add a title and to draw and color a picture.

Second Word Bank

movie theater • movie • cartoon • film • popcorn seller • soda • seat • roller coaster ride • adventure

Name _____ Date _____

Write a story about the picture using some of the words in the first word bank, but make the words plural. Some nouns that end in the letters *s, ch, sh, ss, x,* or *z* add the letters *es* to show more than one (for example, fox/foxes, glass/glasses, and branch/branches). For nouns that end in the letter *y* without the vowels (*a, e, i, o, u*) in front of them, change the *y* to *i* before adding *es* (for example, party/parties). Do not forget to add a title and to draw and color a picture.

First Word Bank

lady • class • mommy • box • penny • bench • story • bus • city • princess • circus • sky • dress • bush

Title: _____

_____

_____

_____

_____

_____

 Writing Extension   In the second word bank, you will see nouns that have special changes when they are plural. On a separate sheet of paper use some of the singular and plural nouns below to write a story. Be sure to add a title and illustrate your story with a picture.

Second Word Bank

man/men	woman/women	child/children
mouse/mice	tooth/teeth	ox/oxen
goose/geese	foot/feet	

Write a Story 1–3, published by Good Year Books. Text Copyright © 1998 Linda Beth Polon.

Name _____ **Date** _____

Possessive nouns are nouns (persons, places, or things) that tell who or what has or owns something. (For example, Mickey has a friend/Mickey's friend) An apostrophe (') and the letter s must be added when a singular noun has or owns something (for example, the dog's leash). Look at the picture and write a story with possessive nouns. Be sure to add a title and illustrate your story.

Title: _____

_____

_____

_____

_____

_____

_____

_____

 Writing Extension   On another sheet of paper, write a story with plural possessive nouns (for example, The cats had kittens/The cats' kittens). In plural nouns, the apostrophe goes after the letter s (for example, trees' leaves, boys' books, teachers' cars). An exception to this rule is when the apostrophe comes before the s in plural nouns such as *men's*, *women's*, and *children's*. Do not forget to add a title and draw and color a picture to illustrate your story.

Name _____ **Date** _____

Contractions are short words that are formed when two words are combined (for example: was not/wasn't, is not/isn't, and are not/aren't). To make a contraction with *not*, you usually can join the verb with the word *not* and replace the *o* in *not* with an apostrophe (for example, did not/didn't). To make other contractions, you'll have to memorize which letters to take out. Here's a list to get you started:

I have/I've, will not/won't, they are/they're, I am/I'm, there is/there's, here is/here's, it is/it's, you are/you're, we have/we've, does not/doesn't, can not/can't

Below the words in the first word bank, write each word's contraction. Using some of these contractions, write a story with a title based on the picture below. Continue on a separate piece of paper.

First Word Bank

had not • did not • were not • should not • would not • will not • are not • I have • there is

Title: _____

_____

_____

_____

_____

_____

_____

Write a Story 1-3, published by Good Year Books. Text Copyright © 1998 Linda Beth Polon.

 Writing Extension On another piece of paper, form the words in the second word bank into contractions and then use some of them in a story. Follow the guidelines above.

Second Word Bank

has not • could not • can not • does not • I am • they are • is not • it is

Name _____ **Date** _____

Abbreviations are short words or letter combinations made from longer words, such as days of the week (Monday/Mon.), months (August/Aug.), places (street/st.), and states (California/CA).

Look at the picture and write a story with a title. Use some of the full words from the word bank to help write your story. Afterward, at the end of your story, write the abbreviation for each word bank word you used. Finish on another piece of paper.

Word Bank

Sunday	Sun.	January	Jan.
Monday	Mon.	February	Feb.
Tuesday	Tues.	March	Mar.
Wednesday	Wed.	April	Apr.
Thursday	Thurs.	August	Aug.
Friday	Fri.	September	Sept.
Saturday	Sat.	October	Oct.
		November	Nov.
		December	Dec.

Alabama	AL	Indiana	IN	Nebraska	NE	South Carolina	SC
Alaska	AK	Iowa	IA	Nevada	NV	South Dakota	SD
Arizona	AZ	Kansas	KS	New Hampshire	NH	Tennessee	TN
Arkansas	AR	Kentucky	KY	New Jersey	NJ	Texas	TX
California	CA	Louisiana	LA	New Mexico	NM	Utah	UT
Colorado	CO	Maine	ME	New York	NY	Vermont	VT
Connecticut	CT	Maryland	MD	North Carolina	NC	Virginia	VA
Delaware	DE	Massachusetts	MA	North Dakota	ND	Washington	WA
Florida	FL	Michigan	MI	Ohio	OH	West Virginia	WV
Georgia	GA	Minnesota	MN	Oklahoma	OK	Wisconsin	WI
Hawaii	HI	Mississippi	MS	Oregon	OR	Wyoming	WY
Idaho	ID	Missouri	MO	Pennsylvania	PA		
Illinois	IL	Montana	MT	Rhode Island	RI		

Title: _____

_____

_____

_____

Name _____ **Date** _____

Writing a letter to a friend or family member is fun. Look at the example letter, and then write one of your own on a separate piece of paper.

(**date the letter**) October 7, 1999

(**greeting**)
Dear Bow Wow, (put a comma after the greeting)

I miss your barks. Have you chased any cats lately? I like cats, but don't tell anyone. Have you gotten any new dog toys? I got a new red collar and leash. Do I look good walking down the street! I get a lot of howls. Write soon.

Love, (Put a comma after the closing of your letter [other closing words: Your friend, Sincerely, Yours truly, Fondly, With love, etc.].)

(Don't write too close to the edges of your paper; leave margins, empty space, around your letter.)

Moochie the Paw

Writing Extension On a separate piece of paper, write a real letter to a cousin, aunt, uncle, grandfather, grandmother, or godmother. Mail it and see if you get a reply. If you do, examine it for proper letter style.

Write a Story 1-3, published by Good Year Books. Text Copyright © 1998 Linda Beth Polon.

Communication

Name _____ **Date** _____

Now address an envelope for your letter. Look at the example below and then try addressing your own in the space provided.

Write the name of who you are writing your letter to (the addressee) in the middle of the envelope, slightly off to the right. Write your name and address in the upper left-hand corner. This is called the return address.

Sample

Davey the Tabby
116 Mouse Tail Road
Fur Ball City, WA 60321

STAMP

Motley the Cat
1 Kitty Corner Lane
Litter Box City, CA 90049

Now address your own envelope.

STAMP

Name _____ **Date** _____

When writing a post card, use the same style as when writing a letter, but write your note only on the left side of the card. Use an opening, write your short note, and then use a polite closing and sign your name. On the right side of the post card, address the post card just as you would an envelope. See the previous page for directions on how to write an address.

Post Card Sample

Dear Tweet Tweet,

I'm having a great vacation flying all over California. It's a pretty place, and I've met a lot of different bird friends. I've eaten a lot of food, and I think I have to go on a diet when I return.

Love,

Chirp Chirp

STAMP

Miss Tweet Tweet
65 Perch Seed Road
Cage City, NV 84631

Now write your own post card below.

STAMP

Write a Story 1-3, published by Good Year Books. Text Copyright © 1998 Linda Beth Polon.

Name _____ **Date** _____

What is journal writing? It is like writing in a daily diary telling about what happened to you during the day, what you did, and how you were feeling. Read the examples below and then write your own journal, or diary, for three days.

Diary Sample

Thursday

Dear Journal,

I fell off my chair in class, and everybody laughed at me. At least we had pizza for lunch. I got mad at my sister because she ripped my homework.

Friday

Dear Journal,

Got a home run in kickball. Wow! I played video games with my friend after school. I lost a lot. I hate that.

Saturday

Dear Journal,

I went to the park with my family. We had a barbecue. My hamburger got burned, and my hot dog fell out of my bun, and my dog ate it. I played ball with my sister. Then, my mom, dad, sister, and I walked home. Boy, am I tired!

Date:

Dear Journal,

_____

_____

Date:

Dear Journal,

_____

_____

Date:

Dear Journal,

_____

_____

Journal Writing

Name _____ **Date** _____

Now it is time to write an invitation. An invitation is a short note card that invites friends, family, or anyone to come to something special, such as a birthday party or graduation.

Look at the example below and then write your own invitation to a pretend party of any kind.

Invitation Sample

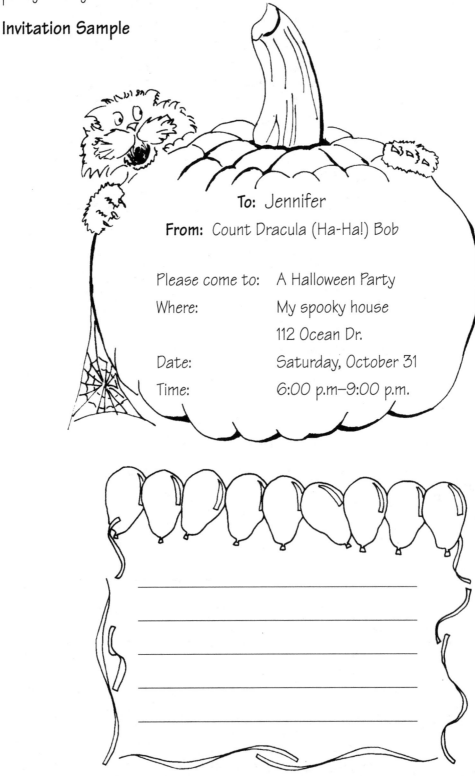

To: Jennifer

From: Count Dracula (Ha-Ha!) Bob

Please come to: A Halloween Party

Where: My spooky house

112 Ocean Dr.

Date: Saturday, October 31

Time: 6:00 p.m–9:00 p.m.

Write a Story 1-3, published by Good Year Books. Text Copyright © 1998 Linda Beth Polon.

Communication

Name _____ **Date** _____

Another type of card is called a thank-you note. Send a thank-you note when someone gives you a present or does something nice for you.

Thank-You Note Sample

Dear Charmaine,

Thank you for my birthday
present. I've wanted that
computer game for a long time.
You are very nice.

Your friend,
Carlos

Now write your own thank-you note below.

Write a Story 1-3, published by Good Year Books. Text Copyright © 1998 Linda Beth Polon.

Communication

Name _____ **Date** _____

Lists are a way to make sure we remember all the things we need to do. Some lists are numbered so they can be completed in order. For example, if you are cleaning up after dinner, you may:

1.   Rinse dishes.
2.   Load dishes in dishwasher.
3.   Put soap in dishwasher.
4.   Turn on dishwasher.

Lists do not need to be numbered if items can be done in any order, such as the things you do to get ready for bed. You can put on your pajamas before or after you brush your teeth, for example.

Write a list, with at least 4 items, for each of the following topics.

Things I'd like to buy at the market.

Jobs or chores I have to do around my house.

Write a Story 1–3, published by Good Year Books. Text Copyright © 1998 Linda Beth Polon.

Communication

Name _____ Date _____

Learning to write directions is important. Well-written directions help people to get from place to place easily. Do you know how to get from where you live to school? Try writing directions from your home to school, even if you take a bus. Don't forget to include street names, places, or landmarks. Write the directions in the form of a numbered list (see the previous page for more information on lists). A sample is given.

Directions Sample

1. Bus picks me up on Emerald Lane.
2. Bus turns left on Grand Avenue.
3. Bus turns right at the light on Grass Lake Road, just past McDonald's.
4. Bus goes up a hill and then turns left on Beck Street.
5. Bus turns right into my school parking lot and lets us out near the big tree.

Beck Street

Grass Lake Road

my school

traffic light

McDonald's

Grand Avenue

my house

Emerald Lane

My Directions from Home to School

1.

2.

3.

4.

5.

6.

 Writing Extension On another piece of paper, draw a map of the route between your home and your school. Also, try writing directions for a new friend to get from school to your house and then draw a diagram.

Name _____ **Date** _____

Look at the boy and girl having a conversation, or dialogue (talking to each other).

Continue their dialogue, using each rule below.

A. Whenever someone is speaking, put quotation marks (" ") around what he or she says. For example: "How are you?" asked Philene.

B. Sometimes writers interrupt the speaker's sentence to let you know who is speaking. For example: "I don't know if I can," said Pedro, "but I'll try." When this happens, be sure to use a comma and end quotation marks after the first phrase and beginning quotation marks at the start of the second phrase.

C. When writing dialogue, you can write the same sentence in more than one way. For example: Denny said, "I love homework." or "I love homework," said Denny.

Finish their conversation.

1. "Did you do your homework?" asked Tommy.

2. "Of course I did," answered Cindy.

3. _____

4. _____

5. _____

6. _____

7. _____

8. _____

9. _____

10. _____

Write a Story 1–3, published by Good Year Books. Text Copyright © 1998 Linda Beth Polon.

Communication

Name _____ **Date** _____

Write a story about the title below, and then draw a picture to illustrate your story. Use some of the words in the first word bank. Also, write a more creative title.

<u>The Dinosaur Swamp</u>

First Word Bank

large • meat eater • gigantic • plant eater •
small • flying • water • swamp • disappear •
friendly • mean • tall • sharp • hungry • nice •
trees • mountains • forest

New Title: _____

_____

_____

_____

_____

_____

_____

_____

_____

_____

 Writing Extension On another piece of paper use the title below and some of the words in the second word bank to write a story. Don't forget to retitle and illustrate your story.

<u>Crazy School</u>

Second Word Bank

classroom • teacher • boys • girls • cafeteria • food • recess • lines • fun •
nurse's office • kickball • yard • principal's office • rules

Storywriting with Prompts

Name _____ **Date** _____

Write a story about the title below, and then draw a picture to illustrate your story. Use some of the words in the first word bank. Also, write a more creative title.

<u>Left Alone in a Toy Store</u>

First Word Bank

computer games • dolls • games • books • action figures • stuffed animals • felt pens • stickers • puzzles • skateboard • balls • fun • exciting

New Title: _____

_____

_____

_____

_____

_____

_____

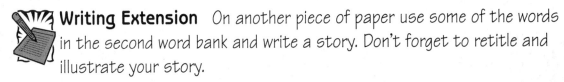 **Writing Extension** On another piece of paper use some of the words in the second word bank and write a story. Don't forget to retitle and illustrate your story.

<u>Market Shopping Spree</u>

Second Word Bank

shopping cart • food • cereal • candy • fruit • bread • desserts • magazines • peanut butter • ice cream • meat • flowers • spaghetti • vegetables • juice

Write a Story 1–3, published by Good Year Books. Text Copyright © 1998 Linda Beth Polon.

Name _____ Date _____

Write a story about the title below, and then draw a picture to illustrate your story. Use some of the words in the first word bank. Also, write a more creative title.

Wild Time at the Amusement Park

First Word Bank

roller coaster • upside down • thrill • fun • fast • exciting • scary • rides • games • tremble • rumble

New Title: _____

_____

_____

_____

_____

_____

_____

_____

_____

 Writing Extension On another piece of paper use some of the words in the second word bank and write your own story. Don't forget to retitle and illustrate your story.

Losing Things at School

Second Word Bank

pencils • erasers • stickers • pencil box • sweater • backpack • lunch box • money • homework • cry • sad • happy • jacket

Name _____ **Date** _____

Write a story about the title below, and then draw a picture to illustrate your story. Use some of the words in the first word bank. Also, write a more creative title.

<u>Homework Again</u>

First Word Bank

like • dislike • responsibility • too • much • reward • learn • fun • feel • good • lose • day

New Title: _____

_____

_____

_____

_____

_____

_____

_____

 Writing Extension On another piece of paper use some of the words in the second word bank and write your own story. Don't forget to retitle and illustrate your story.

<u>If I Ran the Zoo</u>

Second Word Bank

charge • animals • different • look • large • monkeys • lions • deer • alligators • plants • trees • living area • penguins • cute • beautiful • furry • water

Storywriting with Prompts

Write a Story 1–3, published by Good Year Books. Text Copyright © 1998 Linda Beth Polon.

Name _____ Date _____

Use the idea, or theme, below to write a story with a title. Continue on another piece of paper. When you are done, copy the doodle any size onto another piece of paper and then finish it to make it into a picture about your story.

[doodle box with a small curved shape]

Theme: When I grow up I want to be what?

My Title: _____

_____

_____

_____

_____

_____

_____

Writing Extension On another piece of paper, use the theme below to write another story and title. This time make up your own doodle in heavy dark crayon and then finish it into a picture about your story.

Theme: If I could change places with my sister, brother, or a friend, whom would I choose and what would I do?

My Title: _____

Write a Story 1-3, published by Good Year Books. Text Copyright © 1998 Linda Beth Polon.

Name _____ **Date** _____

Use the idea, or theme, below to write a story with a title. Continue on another piece of paper. When you are done, copy the doodle any size onto another piece of paper and then finish it to make it into a picture about your story.

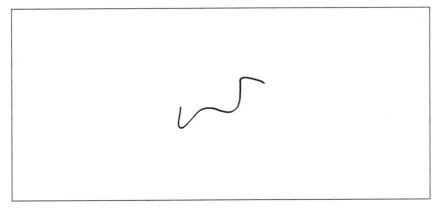

Theme: How my mom/dad likes to spend her/his weekend.

My Title: _____

_____

_____

_____

_____

_____

_____

Writing Extension On another piece of paper, use the theme below to write another story and title. This time make up your own doodle in heavy dark crayon and then finish it into a picture about your story.

Theme: What makes a friend a best friend?

My Title: _____

Write a Story 1–3, published by Good Year Books. Text Copyright © 1998 Linda Beth Polon.

Name _____ **Date** _____

Use the idea, or theme, below to write a story with a title. Continue on another piece of paper. When you are done, copy the doodle any size onto another piece of paper and then finish it to make it into a picture about your story.

Theme: If I could travel anyplace, where would I go?

My Title: _____

_____

_____

_____

_____

_____

_____

Writing Extension On another piece of paper, use the theme below to write another story and title. This time make up your own doodle in heavy dark crayon and then finish it into a picture about your story.

Theme: If I were the teacher of this class, what would I do?

My Title: _____

Name _____ **Date** _____

Use the idea, or theme, below to write a story with a title. Continue on another piece of paper. When you are done, copy the doodle any size onto another piece of paper and then finish it to make it into a picture about your story.

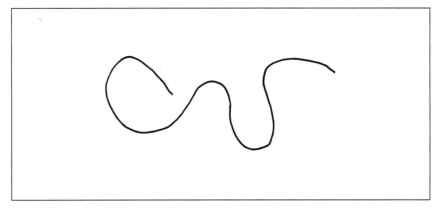

Theme: I woke up one morning, and I was as small as a cookie.

My Title: _____

_____

_____

_____

_____

_____

_____

Writing Extension On another piece of paper, use the theme below to write another story and title. This time make up your own doodle in heavy dark crayon and then finish it into a picture about your story.

Theme: What would happen if for one day you were magically turned into a boy (if you're a girl) or a girl (if you're a boy)?

My Title: _____

Write a Story 1-3, published by Good Year Books. Text Copyright © 1998 Linda Beth Polon.

Name _____ **Date** _____

Use the idea, or theme, below to write a story with a title. Continue on another piece of paper. When you are done, copy the doodle any size onto another piece of paper and then finish it to make it into a picture about your story.

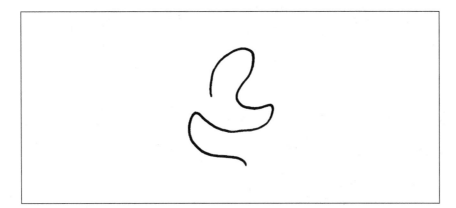

Theme: Name four or more things you'd like to be that aren't human or animal and why.

My Title: _____

_____

_____

_____

_____

_____

_____

 Writing Extension On another piece of paper, use the theme below to write another story and title. This time make up your own doodle in heavy dark crayon and then finish it into a picture about your story.

Theme: What animals I'd like to be and why.

My Title: _____

Name _____ Date _____

Use the idea, or theme, below to write a story with a title. Continue on another piece of paper. When you are done, copy the doodle any size onto another piece of paper and then finish it to make it into a picture about your story.

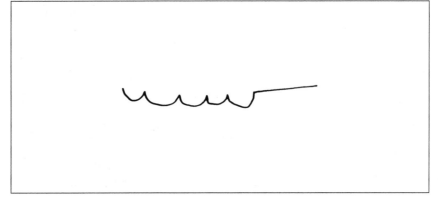

Theme: What I'd do if my friend lost his or her pet.

My Title: _____

_____

_____

_____

_____

_____

_____

Writing Extension On another piece of paper, use the theme below to write another story and title. This time make up your own doodle in heavy dark crayon and then finish it into a picture about your story.

Theme: I woke up invisible, and what a day I had!

My Title: _____

Write a Story 1–3, published by Good Year Books. Text Copyright © 1998 Linda Beth Polon.

Storywriting with Prompts

Name _____ **Date** _____

The first part of the sentence below **begins** a story. Read it and then write the rest of the story. Continue your story on another piece of paper, if necessary. Illustrate your story in the box below.

Title: _____

There was a loud noise in my house, and I _____

_____

_____

_____

_____

_____

_____

_____

Name _____ **Date** _____

The first part of the sentence below **begins** a story. Read it and then write the rest of the story. Continue your story on another piece of paper, if necessary. Illustrate your story in the box below.

Title: _____

It happened in class, and I couldn't stop laughing because _____

_____

_____

_____

_____

_____

_____

_____

Write a Story 1-3, published by Good Year Books. Text Copyright © 1998 Linda Beth Polon.

Name _____ **Date** _____

The first part of the sentence below **begins** a story. Read it and then write the rest of the story. Continue your story on another piece of paper, if necessary. Illustrate your story in the box below.

Title: _____

My eyes almost popped out as I stared at my tray lunch at school and found

a _____

_____

_____

_____

_____

_____

_____

Name _____ **Date** _____

The first part of the sentence below **begins** a story. Read it and then write the rest of the story. Continue your story on another piece of paper, if necessary. Illustrate your story in the box below.

Title: _____

I was on a field trip with my class when suddenly I got lost, so I _____

_____

_____

_____

_____

_____

_____

_____

Write a Story 1-3, published by Good Year Books. Text Copyright © 1998 Linda Beth Polon.

Name _____ **Date** _____

The first part of the sentence below **begins** a story. Read it and then write the rest of the story. Continue your story on another piece of paper, if necessary. Illustrate your story in the box below.

Title: _____

When I was at the zoo, all the animals jumped out of their homes and _____

_____

_____

_____

_____

_____

_____

_____

Name _____ **Date** _____

The first part of the sentence below **begins** a story. Read it and then write the rest of the story. Continue your story on another piece of paper, if necessary. Illustrate your story in the box below.

Title: _____

A strange thing happened the other day in the toy store when I changed into a toy and _____

_____

_____

_____

_____

_____

_____

_____

Write a Story 1–3, published by Good Year Books. Text Copyright © 1998 Linda Beth Polon.

Storywriting with Prompts

Name _____ **Date** _____

The first part of the sentence below **begins** a story. Read it and then write the rest of the story. Continue your story on another piece of paper, if necessary. Illustrate your story in the box below.

Title: _____

I was playing in the schoolyard when suddenly I grew taller than the school

building, and I _____

_____

_____

_____

_____

_____

_____

_____

Name _____ **Date** _____

The first part of the sentence below **begins** a story. Read it and then write the rest of the story. Continue your story on another piece of paper, if necessary. Illustrate your story in the box below.

Title: _____

While I was watching television, something pulled me into the TV set, and I _____

_____

_____

_____

_____

_____

_____

_____

Name _____ **Date** _____

Read the sentence below that **ends** a story, and then write the beginning of the story that leads up to this last sentence. Continue your story on another piece of paper, if necessary. Illustrate your story in the box below.

Title: _____

It scared me, but I was brave.

_____

_____

_____

_____

_____

_____

_____

_____

Name _____ **Date** _____

Read the sentence below that **ends** a story, and then write the beginning of the story that leads up to this last sentence. Continue your story on another piece of paper, if necessary. Illustrate your story in the box below.

Title: _____

This was the luckiest day of my life!

_____

_____

_____

_____

_____

_____

_____

_____

Write a Story 1-3, published by Good Year Books. Text Copyright © 1998 Linda Beth Polon.

Name _____ **Date** _____

Read the sentence below that **ends** a story, and then write the beginning of the story that leads up to this last sentence. Continue your story on another piece of paper, if necessary. Illustrate your story in the box below.

Title: _____

Now I know how to be a good friend.

_____

_____

_____

_____

_____

_____

_____

_____

_____

_____

Name _____ **Date** _____

Read the sentence below that **ends** a story, and then write the beginning of the story that leads up to this last sentence. Continue your story on another piece of paper, if necessary. Illustrate your story in the box below.

Title: _____

I was happy my wish came true for my best friend and me.

_____

_____

_____

_____

_____

_____

_____

_____

```
┌─────────────────────────────────────────────────┐
│                                                   │
│                                                   │
│                                                   │
│                                                   │
│                                                   │
│                                                   │
│                                                   │
└─────────────────────────────────────────────────┘
```

Storywriting with Prompts

Write a Story 1–3, published by Good Year Books. Text Copyright © 1998 Linda Beth Polon.

Name _____ **Date** _____

Read the sentence below that **ends** a story, and then write the beginning of the story that leads up to this last sentence. Continue your story on another piece of paper, if necessary. Illustrate your story in the box below.

Title: _____

My teacher helped me feel proud about what I did today.

_____

_____

_____

_____

_____

_____

_____

_____

_____

Name _____ **Date** _____

Use these sentences for the **middle** of a story. Write the beginning and ending for your story and add a title. Continue your story on another piece of paper, if necessary. Illustrate your story in the box below.

Title: _____

After the spaceship landed, I was calm. Then, the spaceship rattled and shook and I became scared.

_____

_____

_____

_____

_____

_____

_____

Write a Story 1-3, published by Good Year Books. Text Copyright © 1998 Linda Beth Polon.

Name _____ **Date** _____

Use these sentences for the **middle** of a story. Write the beginning and ending for your story and add a title. Continue your story on another piece of paper, if necessary. Illustrate your story in the box below.

Title: _____

"The worst part of the storm will be here by noon," our teacher said.

_____

_____

_____

_____

_____

_____

_____

_____

_____

_____

Name _____ **Date** _____

Use these sentences for the **middle** of a story. Write the beginning and ending for your story and add a title. Continue your story on another piece of paper, if necessary. Illustrate your story in the box below.

Title: _____

The tickets I'd always dreamed of having were now mine.

_____

_____

_____

_____

_____

_____

_____

_____

Write a Story 1–3, published by Good Year Books. Text Copyright © 1998 Linda Beth Polon.

Storywriting with Prompts